gone to the edges

gone to the edges

Leon de Kock

Protea Book House
Pretoria
2006

gone to the edges
Leon de Kock
First edition, first impression 2006

Protea Book House
PO Box 35110, Menlo Park, 0102
1067 Burnett Street, Hatfield, 0083
protea@intekom.co.za

Typography by Hond CC
Graphic material on cover by Celéste Burger
Printed and bound by ABC Press

ISBN 1-86919-132-3

© 2006 Leon de Kock
© All rights reserved.
No part of this book may be reproduced in any form,
without prior permission in writing from the publisher.

I   **After the death of marriage: 2003–2004**

    I have gone to the edges — *9*
    Groundless ground — *10*
    Gedig vir mans, oor verslawing — *12*
    So, the gloves are off, now — *13*
    They dug up your garden — *14*
    Hulle't jou tuin omgedolwe — *15*
    The bridges — *16*
    Stukkend — *17*
    The gutters never work — *18*
    Wife, departed — *19*
    Punctuation — *21*
    The endlessness — *22*
    Lift it clean — *23*
    Non serviam — *24*
    Lamb to the slaughter — *25*
    Why he hates her — *26*
    Russian time — *27*
    Grapefruit — *28*
    The deep guts — *29*
    Empty — *30*
    Leeg — *31*
    Daemon — *32*
    Strong feelings — *33*
    The eye — *34*
    Like a stone — *36*
    Love-notes — *37*
    Sms poems — *38*
        1 Yr appetite
        2 foot by foot
        3 Fishnetted
    Manifesto — *41*

II From the inside: 1998–2002

The child looks with pity — 47
Fifteen years of fame — 48
Father and son — 49
Scientist of my moods — 51
The percussion of schizophrenia — 52
Bird, trapped — 53
Everything you don't yet know — 54
Deep inside my heart — 56
I must go now — 58
Surf — 59
When you finally tip over — 60
Drifting — 61
A bend in the river — 62
'n Lekker klein pakkie — 63
The wall — 64
Deep river — 65
Winter night — 66

I
After the death of marriage: 2003–2004

I have gone to the edges

I have gone to the edges
the many edges
and now I'm half-falling
half-standing
crouching to let my blood
catch my head.
I've seen the allegory
man and woman
coupling
unclasping
pacing the measure
the distance they can bear
the touch they can afford
and I have seen her
danced with the Girl from Ipanema
tilted on that mouthwetting
foretaste of the forever slipping
trick with desire
and I have tasted
the mouth-stopped excess
from which
we have no choice
but to recover
and rediscover
breath.

Groundless ground

The groundless ground
grinding and swaying
nothing to hold
everything to grasp
little to stay
everything to say
and how to speak
and with what voice
and what audience.

Surfaces come into sight
glancing shimmers
shafts of delight
the scent of musk
smell of curved skin
in a nape of neck
a cleft of feeling:
it floats
into the morning sun.

My head, my hands
my bowl of flesh
from which I pick
these restless snacks
drive down the pleasures
drive them deep home
and come up for air

with what hands
will I take the world

guide my hands
let them hold
let them hold

curve the air
make the ground dance

and the body be held
in reverence

reverence of earth
and miraculous engineering
body and being.

Gedig vir mans, oor verslawing

Die begeerte na vroue
draai in ons soos die kolk
van verslawing
en vroue spring ook
diep in die dwarreling in,
dit wil sê, as hulle lus kry,
as die delikate drif
ontboesem word:
versierde woestheid,
barokke eenvoud.

Die begeerte na vroue
proe soos die tuit van verslawing
die diep, keelaf-smaak
van Laphroaig
sylangs-soete moeras
skop-in-die-maag
soos 'n kont wat oop lê en wag.

Ons begeer mekaar
soos hulpelose verslaafdes,
soveel het ek al vasgestel:
die begeerte om niks meer te kan hoor,
om ons gemoedere met 'n lus te deurboor.

So, the gloves are off, now

So, the gloves are off, now.
It was always a bloody business
Always a cracked skull
A bicycle-spoke between the ribs.
But we tried to talk it nice
Talk it into the shape of concept:
"Self-exploration." "Discovery."
Actually, it was a slow dying
Death of the one intimacy
The one that permits no other
The one that kills flies
Should they buzz too close
Too close to the ooze and flow
That most corrupt scent
The invitation to one man.
One man only.

They dug up your garden

They dug up your garden
The bastards
They just shovelled a trench
Right through it
Plumbers. Shitworkers.
They unblock the pipes
They locate the rust
The ruptures
Deep under your roses
Your white radiance.

I shouted at them
I ranted and remonstrated
But there it lay:
A stinking trench
Just below your line of defence
Your icy beauty
It was always there.

Hulle't jou tuin omgedolwe

Die fokkers!
Hulle't jou tuin omgedolwe
'n Loopgraaf gemaak
Strykdeur
Loodgieters. Kaksoekers.
Op soek na kneusplekke
Breekpunte
Diep onder jou rose
Jou wit skynsel.
Ek't hulle berispe
Geskree en gevloek
Maar kyk:
'n Vrot gat
Digby jou verskansing
Jou kil skoonheid
Dit het nog altyd
Gelê en wag.

The bridges

The bridges
Back to our love
Blown up
Bodies lie scattered
Blood everywhere

Stukkend

Bewildered
Verwilderd
Los en vas
Lost and found
Pulled apart
Bits and pieces
Stuksgewys
This way then that way
Lekker stukkend

The gutters never work

The gutters never work
When the real storm comes
They just burst over
Spilling water
That will not flow
In the manner for which
Gutters were designed.
Gutters all, always blocked.
Gutted, stopped with humus
Rotted rich mulch
The stuff that lays up
That lays up and sinks and grows
While elsewhere human life gathers.
An unruly gathering
Rot and hope
That rich earthsour savour
And all the while
The gutters stop up
Until
The
Storm
Bursts.

Wife, departed

We both loved words
words like stones
in the palms of our hands
some grainy, some rough,
some smoothly finished
with the glint of a tiger's eye
others carrying sea-grain
shaped like the caresses of waves.

We both loved the feel
between our fingers
the grain against our skin.
We could play with words
toss them about lightly
always catching their fall
in that net of our mutual
intelligence.

Which is why I was so shocked
when I saw, disbelievingly,
you had taken the dictionary,
that touchstone of our minds
when you moved out
of my now cave-like house.

Later, I found it.
You hadn't taken our tome
our tomb of words
after all.
And I was reminded
how sweet
how bittersweet
is the tang of your reticence.

Punctuation

It's punctuation
said Ricky (PhD, psychotherapist)
It marks a crisis
Your Map of the World
Running up against
The Blueprint.
Punctuation, yes
A comma
Like a purple gouge
White-cutting
Skin & flesh
And then the droplets
The slow seeping
The blood.

The endlessness

After the flood
The residue
The riverbed strewn
Swept-down smashed bits
Nothing goes away completely
They break and hold
Hold and harden
Dry out in the sun
Days like dreams
Nothing changes
Everything shifts
The broken bits harden
Like glass they glint
Like shards they glitter
Ready to cut
Do nothing but wait
See out the endlessness
A terrible duel with time.
After the flood
The residue
After the flood
The rest of time.

Lift it clean

Like a hand
Ripping a heart out
That's what it is
That's what it amounts to
Deep dark pleasures
Desperate pleasures of the flesh
They breed their own pestilence
A virus called unease

Disease

Easy now
Easy baby

Lift it clean
Clean out of the blood

Non serviam

I will not
Be the pickings
In the gaps
Between your teeth.

I will not
Be left to rot
Be left to smell
The shame
Of abandonment.

I will gather up
My bits and pieces
And militate
Against your teeth.

Lamb to the slaughter

I will not play the lamb in wolf's clothing

There is blood dripping from my chops
I have been eating my own heart

You are going to have to make do
Without my conversation.

Why he hates her
(After Leonard Cohen)

She took his heart
and she butchered it
but not before
many years
of seasoning
that's what makes him hate her
the most, the shit fuck.
She pickled his heart
over many years
softened it in brine
and then
when she took her carving knife out
it separated like lamb's meat
it tore apart like cottonwool
that's why he hates her
as much as he once thought
he loved her.

Russian time

One moment:
Time will never pass
Innocently
Things
Will happen

Grapefruit

Grapefruit
like crimson
grapeshot
blood spreading
a badge
for the beauty
of mortal radiance.

The deep guts

Leather jacket crumpled
Over a chair
Lamplight caught
In a jug of water
Golden whisky wave
In the guts
The deep guts.

Late-night amber
Body's downfall
Spirit's uplift
There's no levelling
No equalling
It's all soft, decaying
And beautiful

Empty

This is just to say:
You have eaten the plums
The fridge is empty

Leeg

Al wat ek wil sê:
Jy't die pruime geëet
Die koskas is leeg

Daemon

Cradle a cup of tea in your hands
Sit in the blow and glare of elements.
They return like the tides of dreams
The dreams that wash your daemon back
Back into your arms that would be free.

Resisted, denied, foresworn, still she comes
In the folds of dreams
In the time of thick surrender
In the forested growth, the lush vines
The echoing valleys of something lost.

And you know you must sit here
Always you must cradle this cup
Always you must sit before the tides.
Hold to your heart the daemon's spectre.
She who haunts your heart with something lost.

Strong feelings

Like shoals of fish
Massed like caviar
Compacted
Slipping the ranks
The squirming mass
Battalions
Feelings
Like bamboo shoots
Like Sunday cricket
Burnished sundowner
Whisky amber
Vermillion
Black tar

The eye

We craned our necks
staring into the eye
of the back garden
walking the forested lane
a river splashing green
between houses and koppie.

It was like staring
into a secret.
Who knows what
wild heart
lurks in that domestic
cultivation?

"It's like looking
into someone's eyes,"
you said. "You know,
that sudden fear
of what may find there."

And then came the dog
shrieking his alarm
like Cerberus:
"Don't enter lightly here.
we have been assailed before,
our hearts have been ransacked,
our gods thrown about
with disdain."

Later, up on the koppie
away from the soft
centre of the eye,
the back garden
wanting to spill its
jewel-box secrets

Cerberus joined us,
no longer guarding
his squared circle,
that domesticated beauty

And other dogs joined us too
seeking our company
as we picked our way
through black-stubbed
monkey-tail bushes & bitter aloes
and abandoned makeshift fireplaces

Where there is nothing left
to protect

And we felt good,
very good.
The dogs felt good, too.

Like a stone

Time
Heavy
In hand
Turn it around
Like a stone

Love-notes

Shoals of SMS's
silvering the air
love-notes
labile currents
hearts astir
transporting air
on electrons of desire

Sms poems

1

Yr appetite
unwinds
under me
uncoils
grows dark
impatient
disregards
probity
convention
whips me
whips me
up
outlives me
thrashes me
into Saturday
three hours
sleep
if I'm lucky.
You take it
with eyes
like hard
imperial gems.
You take it in
the vista:
yr hunger.

2

    foot by foot
     I steel my feet
       so when
          ground
                 falls
    my step will be
        fleet

3

Fishnetted
by yr stockings
blacked-out
on yr boots
lip-sticked
on yr mouth
plunged in
yr bursting bust
legwrapped
around hips
like cream
splashed
as you split
and reconvene
yr feet around
these hip-hop
hips o' mine
hip-hip hooray
oh baby
baby oh
here we go

Manifesto

So – it's all become clear now,
just a simple fact.
I live in wilderness chasm
where the buffeting is strong,
pure, unsure. I work my talents
and forge a rough home
in the winds, knowing
there are no false comforts
and no cages of order
through which gales blow
anyway. The caged canary
has lost his sweet bluff.

No more dark lyrics
from within the hold
while waters suck
at the boards. Now,
like Prometheus, it is time
to take fire in hand,
on the skin, looking
it straight in the eye.
Now is the time to see
around the curve
of this disenchanted horizon,
this horizon of disenchantment.

The bland comforts of home
and marriage, the comforts
that never were
that somehow deceived
the hungering heart
and yielded their quartered
crop halfheartedly
that somehow combined to feed
the hungering heart
with even more hunger,
these have been blown
away, away, anyway
any way you look at it.

And now is the time
to hold up those hungers
to love them and console them
unconsolingly. It is time
to bid farewell to the idea,
the very notion of comfort.
There is work
there is breath
there is accident
it is time to unwake
the little demons
who scream for comfort
for the comfort of creatures,
dogs sleeping on the kitchen floor.

Sit in the stream
the stream of breath.
Move like the wind
in the purposelessness
the dangerous drift of what arises.
Let it not be, let it
be not what you design.

Go there
go to the borderless places.
Yield. Give up,
give up, give up the strong signs
of design.
Here comes the flood.

II
From the inside: 1998–2002

The child looks with pity

The child looks with pity
at the grown-ups

who sit facing each other
with awkward limbs and dry mouths

the snap of joy somehow departed
from their movements

and the quickness of breath
no longer lashing their words

which proceed from their mouths
like the rattle of old seeds

while they cross and uncross their legs
and enquire about each other's health.

Fifteen years of fame

The cooing of doves
And the steadfastness of rock
On a koppie in the Old Transvaal
Certainly outlast 15 years of fame.

The beat of my heart
Systole, diastole, systole, diastole
Inside the cave of my chest
Certainly speaks lessons to me.

It is this: systole, diastole
Systole, diastole, systole, diastole
It is this: today, tomorrow
Today, tomorrow, today, tomorrow.

Father and son

In the middle of your sleep
when you wake up
and your great terror
is your father's anger
because you woke him up
again
your long lashes
sticking together
as you look up at him
because you're crying, apologising
as he looms
comforting you
with a dangerous comforting face
sitting on his pile of rage
because you've woken him up
again
and you've felt that anger whip you before.
In the middle of the night
when this happens
then your father
comes up short
against himself
and he knows
this child is he

and this rage
is against
all the failure
in his short life
his short life.

His short dying life.

Scientist of my moods

Every morning I fight for my life
As I sit down to slow my breathing
My breathing like a branching tree
As I sit down to slow the river

To learn not to teach myself
Save myself from the shape of myself
To soothe the murder in my heart
Perhaps to become the scientist of my moods

So to mix myself into perfected feeling
Flowing into the full river of myself
Never the same, always the same
And drowning myself always, always

Resurrecting myself from the river
Of my drowned days.

The percussion of schizophrenia

His feet track the fever in his brain
For six hours he paces up and down
His mouth firing giggles like a machine-gun.
His mind is a cement-mixer
Each devilish new idea
Contorts his shivering anus.

His head shreds composure
Like a carrot grater.
Unlike the rest of us
He knows the price of ideas
Is feeling them rip him apart.

Bird, trapped

There's a bird trapped in my chimney.
I'm like God:
I can't enter the narrow channel
Where he beats against the walls
And he is the mortal
Who can't see the exit above
Or the big room all around him.

If only he would let himself fall
If only he stopped flying against the walls
If only he let go of his muscles
He would fall to the bottom
Walk free
And I wouldn't be sitting here
Writing a poem about his death.

Everything you don't yet know
(From a father to a son)

Everything you don't yet know
is so much more than you think
so much more than catching a fish
or driving a car, buying a house
being poor, destitute or dead
so very much more.

How can I explain —
when you grow big
you'll actually grow small
and when you get stuff
you'll really just lose it all.

How can I explain —
not having read Freud
you won't know
that everything you think you seem
is but a thumbprint
for what you don't yet know you mean
or never will

that everything you do know
you actually don't —
how can I explain?
The Unconscious?
The Super-Ego? The Id?

No, let me rather just say
that one day you'll go running.
Furiously you'll run down a quiet street
and then you'll shout from the pit of your stomach:
"Fuck Oedipus! Fuck Oedipus!"

Deep inside my heart

In the deep heart of sleep
I dream of being lured away
by an old lover
gone now but always wanting me
the way I am always wanting now
and we are taken down into rank
wet wrenching union
the smell of bodyweed
from which I suddenly want to escape
and I ask her was there a child
and she cries and says yes yes yes there was
and I wake in my dream
to the knowledge
that I'm dreaming
and I thrash against the folds of this dream
it becomes a dream in which I know
I am held from my other life
by this life of blame and betrayal
grief and guilt
and I twist and groan and struggle until
I wake again
To my wife who says it's OK
I've been nursing you these last two weeks
you've been very ill
and then finally

I am back in the dark hot night
my wife resistantly asleep next to me
her neat buttocks and shining thighs exposed to
the air
her breathing deep and close
and I sink to that level of waking stillness
when the body feels like a stone
at the bottom of a clear clear pond
from where it sees everything swirling
or resting and it knows
certain movements are possible
but now it simply wishes
to rest under its own weight.

I must go now

I must go now

into the well of the sudden night
where my wife lies, out of sight.

Down the passage, to the left
my darkness awaits me, like a cleft.

Surf

Suddenly
wet at the loins
still entwined
that grating roar
the memory of surf
blooms like a flower

When you finally tip over

When you finally tip over
Spilling a hungry flesh smell
That tastes like the nape of your neck
And when your lips finally part
Upon mine, and I taste the wild garden
You have held back from sight
All day, all day long
Then a river breaks inside me
And it washes with it my wrack
My tangled skeins and bitter threads
And my clotted gut uncoils
As the river of white melting
Flows in me like dissolving words
Inside my disappearing body
As you wash me away
Wash me
Away.

Drifting

The leaves drift sideways, slowly.
They could remain there, almost
forever. They drift like the things
in a mind: dark, definite, forgetful

until you decide to rake them up
an act of housekeeping
relieving the burden when
clots and heaps converge.

Today they're at the bottom of the pool.
Their drift is dreamy and lethargic.
My housekeeping is unthinking:
it does not matter how many leaves are left.

What matters is the act of cleaning
and the shiftless persistence of leaves
and the forgetting amid the clearing
and the simple rhythm of back and forth

and then, and more, and then, and more.
I realise — and soon forget —

my history is a drift of leaves.

A bend in the river
(For Luke, Groot Marico, July 1998)

No matter that fields of stubble chafe
the trees crowding up against the bank
no matter that hills of baleful dust
fall back upwards, choking on stones
no matter the thorns, the chickens
the masters and servants, their deportments.

It's the bend in the river that slips, that slips
the mind and its clicking cogs, the curve
that reaches into a recumbent beyond
a mirror of itself darkening out of reach
a river that means nothing
staring down at its own eternity above.

And as we crease this viscous green
shaving our boat past thickets of bamboo
we clear by a hair underwater rocks like teeth
glide past the stumps you think are crocodiles
steal over watery depths which once
swallowed whole the beats of your heart.

We're drifting into a bend in the river
question-marks bent over ourselves.

'n Lekker klein pakkie

Hy stap by sy vriend se kantoor in
en sien terloops op die die e-mail-skerm:
"Hier's 'n lekker pakkie poes vir jou,"
met, onderaan, 'n stuk of ses attachments.

Dink net: 'n downloadable pakkie poes,
rou vlees opgeskep in die ene nulle,
uitgespreek in 'n ligstorm skermpixels
'n sintuiglike simulakrum, met glas tussenin.

En hy wonder, terwyl hy uitstap, self half-
hunkerend vir sy eie klein pakkie poes,
self half-verleë oor die klaarblyklike
exploitative patriarchal male gaze, oftewel die blik,

hy wonder of poes in 'n blik of 'n pakkie
(sonder om te blik of bloos)
'n goeie plaasvervanger is vir poes op die been;
hy wonder watter stuwende oerimpuls
dit is wat poes so lekker maklik kan losmaak

van die hart.

The wall

The man stands at the wall,
writing.
The wall is his life.
He stands and he writes, fervently.
All day, all the days of his life,
his friends & enemies can see the writing
on the wall,
the message he leaves in the wake
of his writing,
the one he struggles his whole life
to see, as he writes, desiring
that his writing should yield
his future,
should unburden his days
of their resistance.
Always, he is looking ahead,
to his next sentence,
and always he leaves the writing
on the wall.

Deep river
(Version of 'Diep Rivier' by Eugène N. Marais)

O Deep River, O Dark Stream,
How much longer must I wait and dream,
The blade of love wrenching my heart?
In your embrace my grief comes apart;
Wash away, O Deep River, the flames of hate,
The great longing always at my gate.
From afar I see the gleam of steel and gold,
I hear the soft rush of water deep and cold;
I hear your voice, whispering in a dream,
Come quickly, O Deep River, O Dark Stream.

Winter night
(Version of 'Winternag' by Eugène N. Marais)

This wind, so cold
    and spare,
This veld, ablaze in
    light so bare,
thrust forth like the mercy of the Lord,
the land reclines, a sharpened sword.
    And high up in the haze,
    scattered in the blaze,
the grass begins to dance
    beckoning the shades.

How sad, how shrill
    the wind's broken beat,
like the cry of a girl
in love with a cheat.
In every curl of grass
    a drop of dew, locked fast.
Quickly it whitens
    to frost like glass.